Welcome Cancer Thriver!

Congrats on downloading this recipe book! Easy and nutritious recipes are such a smart place to start and continue with your cancer recovery and preventing a cancer recurrence. Included here are recipes with simple ingredients, cancer recovery tips, and meals to make your entire family happy.

Maybe you are still struggling with side effects from your treatment:weight gain, hot flashes, exhaustion, joint pain. Maybe you are terrified your cancer will come back. Cancer is still taking up your time and energy! If so, you are in the right place. You are absolutely right in thinking it does not need to be like this forever.

The 100 recipes included here are terrific but you probably know this is just a starting point. If you are ready to see real results in your cancer recovery, you are going to need more support! You're going to need support specific to you and your body. Here's what to do next:

Join the Cancer Freedom Program!

This is a proven, step by step recovery plan, designed for women who have been diagnosed with cancer. If you are ready to close the chapter on cancer, click the link below.

Click HERE
www.cancerfreedomprogram.com

CANCER RECOVERY | EXPERT

Breakfast

Chocolate & Chia Seed
Overnight Oats

Cancer Recovery Tip:
Protein is key for many aspects of cancer recovery - energy, weight loss, building lean muscle. Start your day with a high protein breakfast.

Ingredients

30 g oatmeal
½ cup almond milk
1 tsp chia seeds
1 scoop protein powder

Directions

Mix all ingredients together and place in a sealable container. Place in the fridge for 8 hours.

Remove in the morning and enjoy!

Serves 1

 V

Nutrition Facts

Macronutrients per serving: 265 calories, 30 g protein, 25 g carbs, 11 g fat.

www.cancerfreedomprogram.com

Peanut Butter
Smoothie

Ingredients

2 bananas
2 cups milk
½ cup peanut butter
2 tbsp honey
2 cups ice cubes

Directions

Place all ingredients in the blender and blend until smooth.

Serves 4

Nutrition Facts

Macronutrients per serving:347 calories, 12 g protein, 38 g carbs, 19 g fat

Almond Berry
Pancakes

Ingredients

¾ cup all-purpose flour
½ cup whole wheat flour
¼ cup sugar
2 tsp baking powder
Dash salt
1 large egg, room temperature, lightly beaten
1-¼ cups fat-free milk
2 tbsp butter, melted
½ tsp almond extract
½ cup fresh raspberries
½ cup fresh blueberries

Directions

Combine the flours, sugar, baking powder, and salt in a large bowl. In a small bowl, combine the egg, milk, butter and extract; stir into dry ingredients until moistened.

Pour 1/4 cup of batter onto a greased hot griddle or pan; sprinkle with berries. Turn when bubbles form on top. Cook until the second side is golden brown.

Serves 10 pancakes

Nutrition Facts

Macronutrients per serving: 179 calories, 9 g protein, 20 g carbs, 7 g fat.

Open Faced Egg
Sandwich

Ingredients

4 large egg whites
2 large eggs
2 tbsp parmesan cheese, grated
2 tsp butter, softened
2 slices whole wheat bread, toasted
⅛ tsp dried rosemary, crushed
⅛ tsp pepper

Directions

Heat a small skillet coated with non-stick spray over medium-high heat. Whisk the egg whites, eggs and cheese; add to the skillet. Cook and stir until set.

Spread butter over toast, and top with egg mixture. Sprinkle with rosemary and pepper. Serve immediately.

Serves 2

Nutrition Facts

Macronutrients per serving: 231 calories, 19 g protein, 13 g carbs, 11 g fat

www.cancerfreedomprogram.com

Herbed Spanish

Omelet

Ingredients

1 lb. potatoes, peeled and diced
2 tbsp olive oil
½ cup red onion, diced
2 cloves garlic, minced
4 large whole eggs, lightly beaten
2 egg whites, lightly beaten
2 tbsp fresh parsley, finely chopped
2 tbsp fresh basil and chives, finely chopped
Salt, to taste

Directions

In a large pan, add potatoes. Cover with water. Bring to a boil and cook uncovered for 3 minutes. Remove from heat. Cover and let stand for about 10 minutes or until potatoes are tender. Drain well.

Spray a deep 10-inch skillet with non-stick spray. Add onion and garlic and cook for about 8 minutes, stirring occasionally. Add potatoes and cook for an additional 5 minutes.

Combine whole eggs and egg whites. Stir in parsley, basil and chives. Season with salt if desired. Pour mixture over potatoes in a hot skillet. Reduce heat and cook uncovered for about 10 minutes or until the bottom of the omelet is golden.

 V

Serves: 4

Nutrition Facts

Macronutrients per serving: 240 calories, 11 g protein, 23 g carbs, 12 g fat

Banana Protein
Pancakes

Ingredients

½ cup rolled oats
½ medium banana
½ tsp vanilla extract
1 tsp baking powder
½ tsp cinnamon
1 egg
¼ cup low fat cottage cheese

Directions

Put all ingredients into a blender and blend for about 30 seconds or until smooth.

Place a nonstick skillet over medium heat. Place 1/4 cup of batter into the skillet. Cook until bubbles appear on top. Flip cakes and cook until golden brown.

Serves 3-4 pancakes

Nutrition Facts

Macronutrients per serving: 162 calories, 10 g protein, 21 g carbs, 4 g fat

Lemon & Chia Seed
Parfaits

Cancer Recovery Tip:

If your taste has changed, you are not alone. Many Cancer Thrivers experience taste changes from treatment. Try adding citrus fruits (limes, lemons and oranges) to help brighten up the flavour of a meal.

Ingredients

2 cups reduced-fat plain greek yogurt
1 tbsp honey
2 tbsp lemon juice
2 tsp lemon zest, grated
2 tbsp chia seed
1 tsp vanilla extract
½ cup fresh raspberries
½ cup fresh blueberries

Directions

Combine the first 6 ingredients. Layer half the yogurt mixture into 2 parfait glasses or custard cups. Top with half the berries. Repeat the layers.

Serves 2

Nutrition Facts

Macronutrients: 298 calories, 20 g protein, 45 g carbs, 4.5 g fat.

www.cancerfreedomprogram.com

Baked Eggs

Ingredients

½ red onion, finely sliced
½ yellow pepper, deseeded and sliced
80 g mushrooms, sliced
1 clove garlic, finely diced
1 tsp smoked paprika
400 g can chopped tomatoes
80 g baby spinach
4 medium eggs
Freshly ground black pepper, to taste

Directions

Preheat the oven to 400 F

Spray a non-stick pan with non-stick cooking oil and warm over medium heat. Add the onion and stir for 2 minutes. Then add the peppers and mushrooms and cook for 4-5 minutes, until soft. Add the garlic and sprinkle over the smoked paprika, then stir. Pour over the chopped tomatoes and mix thoroughly. Reduce the heat and simmer for about 8 minutes, stirring occasionally. Then stir through the spinach and cook for 2 minutes, until the mixture has thickened and the spinach has wilted.

Transfer into an ovenproof dish, and using a spoon, make four shallow wells. Break one egg into each of the wells. Season with black pepper and cook in the oven for 10-12 minutes, until the eggs are set, but the yolks are still runny.

Serves 2

Nutrition Facts

Macronutrients per serving:262 calories, 20 g protein, 24 g carbs, 11 g fat

Spring Vegetable
Frittata

Ingredients

5 large eggs
5 egg whites
½ cup parmesan cheese, grated
1 tbsp fresh parsley, chopped
1 tbsp olive oil
½ cup red potatoes, cooked, peeled and cut into ½-inch pieces
¾ cup onions, chopped
½ cup fresh asparagus, cut into 1-inch pieces on the diagonal
Freshly ground pepper to taste
Salt to taste

Directions

Whisk the eggs, egg whites, cheese, parsley, salt and pepper together until thoroughly combined.

In an oven-proof skillet, heat the oil over medium heat. Add the onion and asparagus and cook until the onion is soft and translucent about 5 minutes. Add the potatoes and turn the heat to low. Add the egg mixture (do not stir) and cook over low heat until the eggs are set, about 15-20 minutes. Meanwhile, preheat the broiler.

Place the skillet under the broiler for 30-45 seconds to finish cooking the top.

Serves 6

Nutrition Facts

Macronutrients per serving: 169 calories, 13 g protein, 7 g carbs, 10 g fat

www.cancerfreedomprogram.com

Egg & Veggie
Scramble

Cancer Recovery Tip:
Eggs are a great source of protein. Pairing with vegetables can help bump up the fibre content and keep you fueled through the day.

Ingredients

4 large eggs, lightly beaten
¼ cup fat-free milk
½ cup chopped green pepper
¼ cup sliced green onions
¼ tsp. salt
⅛ tsp pepper
1 small tomato, chopped and seeded

Directions

In a small bowl, combine eggs and milk. Add green peppers, onions, salt and pepper. Pour into a lightly greased skillet. Cook and stir over medium heat until eggs are nearly set, 2-3 minutes. Add tomato; cook and stir until eggs are completely set.

Serves 2

Nutrition Facts

Macronutrients per serving: 173 calories, 15 g protein, 7 g carbs, 10 g fat

Swiss Chard
Frittata

Ingredients

3 lbs raw swiss chard (Yields ~1 lb)
4 tbsp extra virgin olive oil
¾ cup onion, diced
3 Garlic cloves, minced
¾ cup parmesan Cheese, grated
½ tsp fresh ground pepper
12 eggs, large

Directions

Preheat the oven to 350 degrees. Bring a large pot of salted water to a boil.

Wash swiss chard, and remove stems. Cut stems into pieces that will fit into the pot. Cook the stems in boiling water until just tender, about 5 minutes. Rough chop swiss chard leaves and add to the boiling water. Cook until tender, about 5 minutes more.

Drain cooked swiss chard and cool under cold running water.

Heat olive oil in a non-stick oven-proof skillet. Add onions and garlic, then sautee until soft. Add chopped cooked swiss chard and sautee to heat through.

Crack eggs into a bowl, and add salt, pepper and grated cheese. Mix with a fork until eggs are well blended. Pour eggs over swiss chard mixture, and stir to incorporate.

Place pan in the oven and bake for 20 - 30 minutes. Remove from heat and let stand 10 minutes.
Cut into wedges and serve warm.

Serves: 6

Nutrition Facts

Macronutrients per serving:336 calories, 21 g protein, 13 g carbs, 23 g fat

Egg & Spinach
Cups

Cancer Recovery Tip:

If you are feeling sluggish in the afternoon, it may be because you are sensitive to morning carbohydrates. Try a breakfast that is high in protein and low in carbohydrates. Like this one!

Ingredients

1 tbsp olive oil
1 cup red onion, finely diced
1 tsp garlic, minced
4 cups raw spinach, chopped
Pinch of nutmeg, grated
Pinch of fresh ground pepper
4 eggs

Directions

Add olive oil, garlic, spinach, nutmeg, pepper and onion to a sauté pan. Sauté until onions are translucent.

Place 1/4 spinach mixture in a muffin tin. Top with 1 whole egg. Repeat.

Bake at 375 degrees for 12 – 15 minutes.

Serves: 4

Nutrition Facts

Macronutrients per serving: 129 calories, 8 g protein, 6 g carbs, 8 g fat

CopyCat Egg
Bites

Ingredients

3 cups egg whites
1 cup low-fat cottage cheese
½ cup roasted red peppers, diced
1 cup spinach, finely chopped
1 cup low-fat monterey jack cheese, shredded

Directions

Preheat oven to 325 F. Spray silicone egg tray with non-stick spray. Fill a 9x11 baking dish halfway with warm water, then place the egg tray overtop.

Add eggs and cottage cheese to the blender. Blend until well combined and creamy. Divide toppings among egg cups and fill the rest with egg mixture. Bake in the oven for 60 minutes until eggs are set. Remove from egg mold one cool.

Serves 12

Nutrition Facts

Macronutrients: 167 calories, 17 g protein, 2 g carbs, 9 g fat.

www.cancerfreedomprogram.com

Tofu Scramble

Ingredients

8 oz. extra-firm tofu
½ tbsp olive oil
¼ red onion, thinly sliced
½ red pepper, thinly sliced
2 cups kale, loosely chopped

Sauce:
½ tsp sea salt
½ tsp garlic powder
½ tsp ground cumin
¼ tsp chili powder
Water (to thin)
¼ tsp turmeric

Directions

Pat tofu dry. Cover with a paper towel and place a heavy object on top to allow it to drain.

 V

Add dry spices to a small bowl and add water until sauce consistency.

Spray a large skillet with non-stick spray and add onion and red pepper. Season with a pinch of each salt and pepper and stir. Cook until softened. Add kale, season with a bit more salt and pepper, and cover to steam for 2 minutes.

Use a fork to crumble tofu into bite-sized pieces. Add tofu to pan with vegetables. Sauté for 2 minutes, then add sauce. Stir immediately, evenly distributing the sauce. Cook for another 5-7 minutes until tofu is slightly browned.

Serves: 2

Nutrition Facts

Macronutrients per serving:212 calories, 16 g protein, 7 g carbs, 15 g fat

Blueberry Crumble

Ingredients

8 cups blueberries, fresh or frozen
2 tbsp lemon juice
1 cup almond flour
½ cup coconut flour
¼ cup granulated sugar
1 tbsp cinnamon
½ cup almond butter
¼ cup maple syrup

Directions

Preheat oven to 350 F. Spray 9x9 inch baking dish with non-stick cooking spray.

In a mixing bowl, mix blueberries and lemon juice. Spread evenly in the baking dish.

Mix almond flour, coconut flour, sugar, and cinnamon in a separate bowl and mix well. Melt almond butter with maple syrup and add to the dry mixture. Stir until a crumbly texture forms.

Cover the blueberries with the crumble mixture and bake for 25 minutes.

Serves: 8

 V

Nutrition Facts

Macronutrients per serving: 210 calories, 7 g protein, 10 g carbs, 17 g fat

Egg & Avocado
Toast

Ingredients

1 slice whole wheat toast
1 egg, cooked
¼ avocado, sliced

Directions

Spray a small skillet with non-stick spray. Cook egg over medium heat. Toast a slice of whole-wheat bread. Thinly slice avocado and place on toast. Place cooked egg on top.

Serves 1

Nutrition Facts

Macronutrients per serving: 232 calories, 11 g protein, 23 g carbs, 12 g fat

Peach Ricotta
Toast

Cancer Recovery Tip:
Ricotta cheese is an excellent source of protein and fat. A great breakfast choice.

Ingredients

¼ cup low-fat ricotta cheese
1 slice whole wheat toast
1 peach
¾ tsp nutmeg

Directions

Toast a slice of whole-wheat bread. Thinly slice peach. Spread ricotta cheese over toast, add peach slices and sprinkle with nutmeg.

Serves 1

Nutrition Facts

Macronutrients per serving: 223 calories, 11 g protein, 38 g carbs, 3 g fat

Mexican
Breakfast

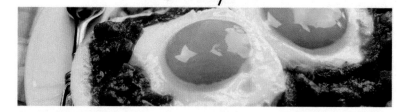

Ingredients

1 (4-ounce) can green chilies
8 ounces ground breakfast
turkey sausage
1 onion chopped
1 red bell pepper, cored and
chopped
1 tsp garlic, minced
1 tbsp chili powder
5 eggs
4 egg whites
2 cups low fat milk
½ cup green onions, chopped
1 ½ cups reduced-fat shredded
Mexican blend cheese
5 x 8-inch flour tortillas, cut
into quarters

Directions

Coat 13x9 inch glass baking dish
with nonstick cooking spray.
Spread green chilies along
bottom of dish.

In a nonstick skillet, cook and crumble
sausage until It starts to brown. Add
onion and bell pepper and cook until
sausage is done and vegetables
tender. Add garlic and chilli powder.
Remove from heat and cool.

In a large bowl, whisk together eggs,
egg whites, and milk, and in another
bowl, combine green onion and
cheese.

Spoon one-third of sausage mixture
over chilies in baking dish. Top with
one-third tortilla quarters and one-third
cheese mixture. Repeat layers, ending
with cheese. Pour egg mixture evenly
over casserole and refrigerate,
covered, for at least 6 hours or
overnight.

Preheat the oven to 350°F. Bake 50-60
minutes or until bubbly and golden
brown.
Serves 10

Nutrition Facts
Macronutrients per serving:262 calories, 18 g protein, 23 g carbs, 7 g fat

Savory Cottage Cheese
Bowl

Ingredients

¾ cup low fat cottage cheese
2 tbsp chives, minced
Freshly ground black pepper
½ cup persian cucumbers,
sliced
½ medium bell pepper, seeded
and chopped
10 grape tomatoes, halved
1 tbsp pistachios, chopped,
roasted, and shelled
Kosher salt, to taste

Directions

In a small bowl, combine cottage cheese
with 1 tablespoon chives and pepper to
taste.

Layer cucumbers, peppers and tomatoes
on top, then garnish with the remaining 1
tablespoon of chives and pistachios.
Sprinkle with a pinch of salt and pepper
to taste.

Serves 1

Nutrition Facts

Macronutrients per serving: 221 calories, 25 g protein, 19 g carbs, 8 g fat.

www.cancerfreedomprogram.com

French Toast
Casserole

Ingredients

8 oz loaf French bread, cut into 1-inch squares
1 (5-ounce) jar seedless all natural blackberry fruit spread
4 ounces reduced-fat cream cheese
2 tbsp sugar
2 tbsp skim milk
1 egg
2 egg whites
¼ cup light brown sugar
1 cup skim milk
1 tsp vanilla extract
½ tsp ground cinnamon

Directions

Coat 9x9 inch baking pan with nonstick cooking spray. Place half of the French bread squares in the prepared baking pan. In a microwave-safe dish, heat jam until melted, stirring. Drizzle over bread.

In a bowl, beat together cream cheese, 2 tablespoons sugar and milk until smooth. Drop over the bread mixture and cover with the remaining French bread squares.

In a large bowl, whisk together egg, egg whites, brown sugar, half-and-half, vanilla and cinnamon. Pour the mixture evenly over the bread. Gently press bread into the liquid mixture, cover, and refrigerate overnight.

Preheat oven 325°F. Bake, covered, 30-35 minutes, uncover 5-10 minutes or until bread is golden.

Serves 6

Nutrition Facts

Macronutrients per serving:184 calories, 7 g protein, 32 g carbs, 3 g fat

Lunch

Burrito Bowl

Ingredients

1 cup mixed greens
¼ cup salsa
4 cherry tomatoes, cut in half
¼ cup canned black beans
100 g ground turkey (or substitute for 100 g seitan for a plant based protein)
1 tsp Tex Mex seasoning
30 g low fat marble cheddar, shredded

Directions

Spray non-stick spray into a frying pan. Add ground turkey and season with Tex Mex seasoning. Cook thoroughly, until browned. Remove from pan.

In small bowl, add mixed greens, cherry tomatoes, black beans, and ground turkey. Top with cheese and salsa.

Serves 1

Nutrition Facts

Macronutrients per serving:438 calories, 39 g protein, 39 g carbs, 14 g fat

Cucumber Tuna
Bites

Ingredients

1 cucumber
¼ cup mayonnaise
1 red bell pepper finely
chopped
4 oz tuna drained
½ tsp smoked paprika
½ tsp garlic powder
¼ tsp salt or to taste
¼ tsp black pepper
⅛ tsp cayenne pepper
optional
red pepper flakes garnish
parsley chopped, garnish

Directions

Cut the cucumber into ½ or ¼ inch bite sizes.

Mix all other ingredients and spices in a bowl, except the garnish.

Taste and adjust for salt.

Scoop the tuna mix and place on cucumber slices.

Garnish with herbs or pepper flakes and serve.

Serves 12.

Nutrition Facts

Macronutrients: 58 calories, 3 g protein, 2 g carbs, 5 g fat.

Carrot Curry
Soup

Ingredients

2 pounds carrots, chopped
3 tbsp olive oil, divided
¾ tsp salt, to taste
1 medium yellow onion, chopped
2 cloves garlic, minced
½ tsp ground coriander
¼ tsp ground cumin
4 cups vegetable broth
2 cups water
1 ½ tsp lemon juice, to taste
Black pepper, to taste

Directions

Toss chopped carrots in 2 tbsp of olive oil and ½ tsp of salt. Roast in the oven at 400°F for 30 min.

In Dutch oven, warm 1 tbsp of olive oil over medium heat. Add chopped onion and ¼ tsp of salt. Cook for 6 min. Add garlic, coriander, and cumin. Pour in vegetable broth and water, while scraping brown bits from the bottom..

Add carrots. Bring to a boil, then reduce heat to maintain a simmer. Cook for 15 min. Remove from heat. Blend untill smooth and add lemon juice and pepper to taste

Serving: 1 cup

 V

Nutrition Facts

Macronutrients per serving: 132 calories, 3 g protein, 17 g carbs, 7 g fat

Black Bean & Corn
Salad

Cancer Recovery Tip:

Mix up your protein sources by choosing a plant-based protein such as soy, legumes, nuts and seeds.

Ingredients

1 tomato, chopped
½ small red onion, chopped
Salt and freshly ground black pepper
¼ cup chopped fresh cilantro
2 (15-ounce) cans black beans, rinsed and drained
1 cup fresh, frozen, or canned no-salt-added corn, drained
2 tbsp fresh lime juice
1 tbsp olive oil
1 tsp ground cumin
1 jalapeño, seeded and finely chopped
1 red, yellow, or green bell pepper, seeded and chopped

Directions

In a bowl, combine black beans, corn, tomato, bell pepper, onion, and jalapeño.

In a bowl, combine lime juice, oil, and cumin and drizzle over bean mixture. Season with salt and pepper and sprinkle with cilantro.

Serves: 8

 V

Nutrition Facts

Macronutrients per serving: 125 calories, 6 g protein, 20 g carbs, 2.5 g fat

www.cancerfreedomprogram.com

Pea & Celery
Soup

Ingredients

1 onion, diced
1 large potato, peeled and diced
4 sticks celery, trimmed and
sliced
3 cups reduced-salt vegetable
stock
3 ¼ cup frozen peas
2 cloves garlic, finely diced
1 red chilli, deseeded and finely
sliced
Small handful fresh mint, leaves
only
Freshly ground black pepper, to
taste

Serves: 4

 V

Directions

Spray a large pan with non-stick spray. Add the onion, potato and celery, and cook for about 3 minutes until the onion has softened.

Add the peas, garlic and chilli, and stir before adding the stock. Bring to the boil, then turn down the heat, cover and simmer for 10 minutes, or until the vegetables are cooked.Stir in mint, saving a few leaves to garnish.

Blend the soup until smooth. Add extra water if needed to give the consistency you prefer.Season with pepper and garnish with the remaining mint before serving.

Serves 4

Nutrition Facts

Macronutrients per serving:166 calories, 9 g protein,30 g carbs, 2 g fat

www.cancerfreedomprogram.com

Chicken Salad
Sandwich

Ingredients

2 skinless chicken breasts
2 tbsp mayonnaise
¼ cup sliced grapes
2 tbsp dried cranberries
¼ cup chopped walnuts
(optional)
2 tsp dried tarragon
8 slices bread

Directions

Preheat oven to 375°F

Roast chicken breasts in oven for
approximately 45 minutes until cooked
through, juices run clear. Cube, dice, or
shred meat.

Add mayonnaise, grapes, cranberries,
walnuts, and tarragon. Mix well and divide
into 4 (~¾ cup) portions and spread onto
bread. Add chicken.

Serves 4

Nutrition Facts

Macronutrients per serving:237 calories, 24 g protein, 13 g carbs, 10 g fat

Carrot Ginger Soup
with Spicy Shrimp

Ingredients

4 cups chopped, peeled, organic carrots
1 cup chopped white onion
½ cup chopped celery
1 tbsp ginger, finely chopped
1 clove of garlic, smashed
1 quart carrot juice
1 quart vegetable stock
¼ tsp chopped tarragon
Salt and pepper, to taste
Few drops sherry vinegar, to taste
4 shrimp (per serving), cooked, peeled, cleaned, chopped
1 pinch of cayenne
Sliced scallions

 V

Directions

Spray a sauce pot with non-stick spray and place over high heat. Add carrots, celery, onion, ginger, and garlic and sauté for 2-3 minutes. Add cayenne, salt, and pepper. Add carrot juice and vegetable stock. Allow liquid to come to a boil then turn heat down and simmer until all vegetables are tender, approximately 30 minutes.

Blend until smooth.

Toss cooked shrimp with cayenne. Place shrimp in bowls. Pour hot soup over and sprinkle with scallions.

Serves: 8

Nutrition Facts

Macronutrients per serving: 285 calories, 30 g protein, 15 g carbs, 12 g fat.

Plant Powered Chickpea
Salad

Ingredients

1 can (15 ounces) chickpeas (garbanzo beans), rinsed
½ cup celery, chopped
½ cup red bell pepper, chopped
¼ cup carrots, chopped
2 tsp garlic, minced
2 tsp fresh dill, minced
2 tsp lemon juice
2 tbsp vegan mayonnaise or avocado
1 ½ tsp yellow mustard
1 tsp nutritional yeast, chopped
2 tsp chili pepper flakes
2 tsp Mrs. Dash or salt
Ground black pepper, to taste

Directions

Pulse drained chickpeas in a food processor.

In a large bowl combine mashed chickpeas with remaining ingredients, mix, and serve with carrot and cucumber slices.

Serves: 6

 V

Nutrition Facts

Macronutrients per serving: 100 calories, 4 g protein, 14 g carbs, 4 g fat

www.cancerfreedomprogram.com

Pesto Toastini

Ingredients

1 cup firmly packed basil leaves
1 cup firmly packed baby spinach
¼ cup blanched almonds
1 tbsp reduced sodium chicken broth
¼ cup lightly packed flat-leaf parsley, stems removed
2 large garlic cloves, chopped
2 tbsp parmesan cheese, grated
3 tbsp extra virgin olive oil
Salt and ground black pepper, to taste
10-12 one-inch whole-wheat bread

Directions

In a food processor, combine the basil, spinach, and parsley. Whirl until the leaves are coarsely chopped. Add the almonds, garlic, cheese and broth. Whirl to a coarse purée With the motor running, gradually drizzle in the oil and process until it is fully blended into the pesto. Season to taste with salt and pepper.

Spread the top of each slice of bread generously with pesto. Heat the pesto-covered slices in a toaster oven until the bread is toasted on the bottom and the pesto is warmed through. Serve immediately.

Serves: 8

 V

Nutrition Facts

Macronutrients per serving: 190 calories, 5 g protein, 25 g carbs, 8 g fat

Chicken Tostadas

Ingredients

1 tbsp cumin
1 tbsp chili powder
1 tsp garlic powder
1 tsp paprika
salt and pepper to taste
1 ¼ pounds chicken breasts, cubed
1 tsp olive oil
1 x 15 ounce can black beans, rinsed and drained
1 tsp garlic, minced
¼ cup fresh cilantro, finely chopped
2 cup cherry tomato, halves
¼ cup red onion, finely chopped
1 large avocado
3 tbsp nonfat plain greek yogurt
2 tbsp lime juice
8 tostada shells
½ cup reduced-fat Mexican blend cheese, shredded

Directions

In small bowl, mix together spices, and season to taste. Toss chicken in seasonings. In large nonstick pan coated with nonstick cooking spray, cook chicken, stirring, until browned and cooked through; set aside. In another bowl, combine tomatoes, red onion, ½ tsp garlic, ¼ cup cilantro and olive oil. Season to taste; set aside. In another bowl, mix beans with remaining ½ tsp garlic; set aside.

In small bowl, mash avocado and add yogurt, lime juice and season to taste, mixing until smooth.

To assemble, spread guacamole on tostada and layer beans, tomato mixture, chicken and cheese.

Serves 8

Nutrition Facts

Macronutrients per serving:297 calories, 23 g protein, 24 g carbs, 12 g fat

www.cancerfreedomprogram.com

Taco Soup

Ingredients

1 pound ground sirloin
2 (10-ounce) cans diced tomatoes and green chilies
1 (15-ounce) can black beans, rinsed and drained
1 (15-ounce) can kidney beans, rinsed and drained
1 (15-ounce) can pinto beans, rinsed and drained
2 (11-ounce) can Mexican style corn, drained
1 (4-ounce) can chopped green chilies, drained
1 (1¼-ounce) package taco seasoning mix
1 (1-ounce) package original ranch salad dressing mix
2 cups water

Directions

In a large nonstick skillet, over medium heat, cook meat until done, 5 minutes.

In 3 1/2 -6-quart slow cooker add cooked meat and all ingredients to pot.
Cook on low for 6-8 hours, or until tender.

Serves 10

Nutrition Facts

Macronutrients per serving: 317 calories, 19 g protein, 37 g carbs, 3 g fat.

www.cancerfreedomprogram.com

Chicken Orzo
Salad

Ingredients

4 cups orzo pasta, cooked
2 cups rotisserie chicken breast, skin removed and chopped
1 cup chopped tomatoes
1 cup frozen corn, thawed
¼ cup red onions, chopped
½ cup green onions, chopped
1 tbsp dijon mustard
2 tbsp lime juice
1 tbsp olive oil
1 tbsp jalapeño pepper, chopped
½ tsp chili powder
½ tsp ground cumin

Directions

In large bowl, combine orzo, chicken, tomatoes, corn, red onion and green onions.

In small bowl, whisk Dijon, lime juice, olive oil, jalapeño, chili powder and cumin. Pour dressing over pasta mixture, tossing to mix.

Serves 8 (1 cup each)

Nutrition Facts

Macronutrients per serving: 258 calories, 17 g protein, 39 g carbs, 4 g fat.

Beet and Toasted Pumpkin Seed Salad

Ingredients

Salad:
4 large beets
¼ cup pumpkin seeds
1 bunch beet greens
2-3 cups arugula leaves, washed and torn into bite-sized pieces
2 scallions, finely chopped

Dressing:
3 tbsp extra-virgin olive oil
2 tbsp balsamic vinegar
¾ tsp Dijon mustard
¼ tsp freshly ground pepper
1 tbsp fresh basil, finely chopped

Directions

Wash beets and remove tops. Place beets in a large pot filled with water and bring to a boil. Lower heat and simmer until beets are tender. Set aside to cool.

Toast pumpkin seeds by placing in a dry skillet over medium heat and stir using a wooden spoon. When seeds begin to smell nutty, remove from the skillet and set aside.

Bring a large pot of water to a boil. Wash beet greens and chop into bite-sized pieces. Drop greens into boiling water and let cook for about 30 seconds. Rinse greens in cold water.

Shake all the dressing ingredients in a jar. Peel beets and cut into small cubes. Squeeze excess water out of the cooked beet greens. Put cubed beets, beet greens, pumpkin seeds, arugula and scallions in a salad bowl. Pour dressing over salad and toss gently.

 V

Serves 6 .

Nutrition Facts

Macronutrients per serving: 150 calories, 8 g protein, 9 g carbs, 11 g fat

Lemon Mustard Salmon
Salad

Cancer Recovery Tip:
Salmon is an excellent option if you are struggling with low appetite.

Ingredients

17 oz canned sockeye salmon, skinless and boneless
3 tsp dijon mustard
2 tsp lemon juice, freshly squeezed
2 tsp extra virgin olive oil
Pinch of cayenne
Pinch of sea salt
3 tbsp celery, finely chopped
2 tbsp fresh parsley, finely chopped

Directions

Put salmon in a bowl and break into small pieces with a fork. Stir in the mustard, lemon juice, olive oil, cayenne, salt, celery, and parsley. If needed, adjust the flavors with lemon juice and a pinch of salt.

Serves 4

Nutrition Facts

Macronutrients: 252 calories, 29 g protein, 2 g carbs, 13 g fat.

www.cancerfreedomprogram.com

Steak & Strawberry
Salad

Ingredients

2 oz top sirloin steak
1 cup spinach
4 strawberries, sliced
30 g low fat goat cheese

Dressing:
1 tbsp balsamic vinegar
1 tbsp mustard

Directions

In frying pan, place top sirloin steak. Cook to desired level. Remove from pan.

In small bowl add spinach, sliced strawberries, and goat cheese. Add sliced and cooked steak.

In small bowl, mix balsamic vinegar with mustard. Drizzle overtop of the salad and serve.

Serving size: full recipe

Nutrition Facts

Macronutrients per serving:208 calories, 18 g protein, 8g carbs, 10 g fat

Big Mac Salad

Ingredients

1 lb extra lean ground beef, browned and
drained
6 cups iceberg lettuce, chopped
1 ½ cup low-fat Colby jack cheese, shredded
1 cup roma tomatoes, diced
1 cup red onion, sliced
½ cup dill pickles, diced
Thousand Island Dressing

Directions

Add chopped lettuce to extra large serving
bowl. Sprinkle cooked ground beef over
lettuce. Sprinkle with cheese, tomatoes,
onion, dill pickles. Toss to combine. Drizzle
with dressing.

Serves 8

Nutrition Facts

Macronutrients per serving: 335 calories, 22 g protein,59 g carbs, 25 g fat

Crunchy Chicken
Salad

Cancer Recovery Tip:
If you are struggling with a low appetite, try to avoid drinking large amounts of fluids right before meals. Instead take small sips of fluids throughout the day.

Ingredients

2 cups (1 med) cubed sweet potato
2 tbsp light mayonnaise
8 oz cooked chicken breast or turkey breast, cubed
1 red bell pepper, cored and seeded, cut into quarters
4 cups salad greens
Salt & pepper, to taste
1 tbsp freshly squeezed lime juice
½ tsp dried thyme leaves

Directions

Preheat broiler. On a lined baking sheet place bell pepper on foil, skin side up. Broil 6-8 inches away from heat source until skin is blackened, about 12 minutes. Let cool slightly and remove skin. Chop coarsely.

In large bowl, toss together pepper, chicken and sweet potato. In a small bowl, stir mayonnaise, lime juice, tarragon, salt and pepper together until blended. Pour over chicken mixture and toss to coat.

Cover and refrigerate at least 2 hours before serving. Serve chicken salad over bed of salad greens.

Serves 4

Nutrition Facts
Macronutrients per serving: 143 calories, 18 g protein, 8 g carbs, 5 g fat

Hawaiian Star
Soup

Cancer Recovery Tip:
Soup is a great way to increase your daily hydration. If you are struggling to drink enough water, incorporate more soups into your diet.

Ingredients

3 tbsp cornstarch
60 oz reduced-sodium chicken broth
2 ribs celery, thinly sliced
3 medium carrots, peeled & thinly sliced
2 tbsp fresh ginger root, grated
¼ cup reduced-sodium soy sauce
1 tsp cayenne pepper, ground
½ tsp chili paste
¼ cup fresh parsley, chopped
1 pound cooked chicken, diced
½ cup uncooked star pasta
black pepper, optional, to taste

Directions

Dissolve the cornstarch in ½ cup cold water in a large stock pot. Add the broth, celery, carrots, ginger, soy sauce, cayenne, chili paste, and 2 cups of water. Simmer for 30 minutes.

Add the parsley, chicken, and pasta; bring the soup to a boil. Cook the pasta as directed on the package and add it to the soup. Garnish the soup with the green onions. Adjust the spiciness with black pepper or more cayenne, if desired.

Serves 6 (1.5 cups each)

Nutrition Facts

Macronutrients per serving: 220 calories, 28 g protein, 18 g carbs, 4 g fat.

Vegetarian Sushi
Bowl

Ingredients

2 tbsp rice vinegar
2 tbsp reduced-sodium tamari
2 tbsp avocado oil
2 tsp toasted (dark) sesame oil
2 tsp grated fresh ginger
2 cups cooked brown rice
1 cup shredded carrot
1 cup diced cucumber
1 avocado, diced
1 cup frozen shelled edamame, thawed
1 cup chopped toasted nori
Sesame seeds for garnish

 V

Directions

Combine rice vinegar, tamari, avocado oil, sesame oil and ginger in a small bowl

Divide brown rice among 4 bowls. Top with equal amounts of carrot, cucumber, avocado, edamame and nori. Drizzle with 2 tbsp dressings each and sprinkle sesame seeds on top, if desired.

Serves 4

Nutrition Facts

Macronutrients per serving:342 calories, 20 g protein, 35 g carbs, 20 g fat

Rainbow Veggie
Wrap

Ingredients

4 (8 inch) multigrain tortillas
or wraps
1 cup prepared olive hummus
2 oz thinly sliced cheddar
cheese
1 ⅓ cups baby spinach
1 cup sliced red bell pepper
1 cup broccoli sprouts
1 cup thinly shredded red
cabbage
1 cup julienned carrots
Green goddess dressing for
serving

Directions

Spread each tortilla with 1/4 cup
hummus. Top each with one-fourth of the
cheddar, spinach, bell pepper, sprouts,
cabbage and carrots. Roll up each wrap.

Slice the wraps into 1-inch rounds. Serve
with dressing for dipping if desired.

Serves: 4

 V

Nutrition Facts

Macronutrients per serving:391 calories, 13 g protein, 40 g carbs, 19 g fat

Greek Chicken
Meatballs

Ingredients

1½ pounds ground chicken
1 cup diced red onion
½ cup feta, crumbled
3 cloves garlic, minced
½ cup parsley, chopped
1 tbsp fresh mint, chopped
(about 8-10 leaves)
2 tsp dried oregano
½ tbsp olive oil
salt and pepper, to taste

Directions

Preheat the oven to 400°F and line a large baking sheet with parchment paper

In a large bowl, mix together the ground chicken, onion, feta, garlic, parsley, mint, dried oregano, olive oil, and salt and pepper until well combined. Try not to over mix. Using a tablespoon, form into meatballs. You should get around 28-30 meatballs depending on the size.

Place on the baking sheet and bake for 25 minutes until golden brown and cooked through. Serve with rice, greek salad, and tzatziki if desired.

Serves 5

Nutrition Facts
Macronutrients per serving:245 calories, 30 g protein, 4 g carbs, 14g fat

No Mayo Tuna
Salad

Ingredients

2 5-oz cans wild-caught tuna, drained
1 cup diced green apple (1/2 large)
1 cup diced red bell pepper
⅓ cup diced red onion
¼ cup parsley, roughly chopped
2 tbsp tahini
2 tbsp lemon juice
Pinch of red pepper flakes
Salt and pepper, to taste

Directions

Add all ingredients to a medium-size mixing bowl and mix to combine. Enjoy as-is, in a salad, on a lettuce wrap, or however you prefer! Store in the refrigerator in a tightly sealed glass container for up to 5 days

Serves 3 cups

Nutrition Facts

Macronutrients per serving:217 calories, 31.5 g protein, 10.5 g carbs, 6.7 g fat

Roasted Cauliflower
Tacos

Ingredients

4 cups cauliflower florets
2 tbsp olive oil
½ tsp Tajin
½ tsp smoked paprika
½ tsp kosher salt
6 street taco size tortillas
pickled red onions, for topping
6 tbsp Peruvian Green Sauce, for topping
sour cream, optional
cilantro, for garnish

Pickled Red Onions:
1 red onion, peeled and sliced into rounds
½ cup apple cider vinegar
1 tbsp cane sugar or maple
1 tsp kosher salt
2 bay leaves

Directions

In a medium bowl combine the cauliflower, olive oil, Tajin, smoked paprika and salt.

Spray the air fryer basket with oil and add the cauliflower, cook at 400°F 12 to 15 minutes until browned and tender, shaking the basket halfway.

In a small saucepan heat the vinegar, water, sugar and salt until it boils and the sugar dissolves.

Transfer onions to a heat safe bowl with the bay leaves and pour liquid over the onions.

Set aside to cool then transfer to a glass jar and refrigerate overnight.

Serves 8

Nutrition Facts

Macronutrients per serving (3 tacos):284 calories, 8.5 g protein, 22.5 g carbs, 3.5 g fat

Supper

Meatballs & Zucchini
Noodles

Ingredients

1 tbsp olive oil
2 small zucchinis
¼ cup white onion, chopped
2 cloves garlic, minced
½ jar pasta sauce
500 g extra lean ground beef
1 tbsp italian seasoning
½ tsp salt
¼ tsp ground black pepper

Directions

Place ground beef into a medium mixing bowl. Add in the Italian seasoning, white onion, garlic, and salt and pepper. Mix and form into meatballs.

Add ½ tbsp of olive oil to pan over medium heat. Add meatballs. Cook until browned on 1 side and then turn.

Once cooked through, remove from pan and set aside.

Wash and cut ends off of zucchini. Use a julienne peeler or spiralizer to cut your zucchini noodles.

Add ½ tbsp of olive oil to same pan and add zucchini noodles. Cook over medium heat stirring infrequently. Once the zucchini noodles soften, add meatballs and pasta sauce over top and cook until warmed.

Serves 4

Nutrition Facts

Macronutrients: 294 calories, 23 g protein, 13 g carbs, 16 g fat.

www.cancerfreedomprogram.com

Turkey Burger

Ingredients

500 g of ground turkey
1 tbsp dried breadcrumbs
½ tsp salt
¼ tsp ground black pepper
¼ tsp garlic powder
¼ tsp onion powder
2 tsp Worcestershire sauce
½ tsp liquid smoke
4 hamburger buns

Directions

In a medium mixing bowl add ground turkey. Add breadcrumbs and all spices. Mix with wooden spoon. Use your hands to mold into 4 burger patties.

Spray pan with non-stick spray. Place burger patties into pan. Cook over medium heat until browned on one side and then flip. Cook through and remove from heat.

Serve on hamburger bun. Add desired toppings (lettuce, tomato slice, low fat mayo, mustard, low fat cheese).

Serves 4

Nutrition Facts

Macronutrients per serving:263 calories, 23 g protein, 24 g carbs, 8 g fat

Brussel Sprout
Salad

Ingredients

½ tbsp olive oil
1 lb brussel sprouts, trimmed and cut in half
4 slices of turkey bacon
120 g low fat smoked cheddar
1 tbsp Calorie Free Syrup
Salt and pepper, to taste

Directions

On a foil lined baking sheet spread out trimmed and cleaned brussel sprouts Drizzle with olive oil.

Cook in the oven at 400 degrees F until softened and edges are browned

While brussel sprouts are baking, cook turkey bacon in pan or air fryer until crispy brown. Let cool and crumb apart using hands. Cut cheese into small cubes.

Place cooked brussel sprouts into a mixing bowl. Add turkey bacon and cheese. Drizzle with Walden Farms Syrup and sprinkle with salt and pepper.

 V

Serves 4

Nutrition Facts

Macronutrients: 159 calories, 11 g protein, 11 g carbs, 9 g fat.

www.cancerfreedomprogram.com

Sweet Chicken
Curry

Ingredients

4 chicken breasts

Marinade:
3 tbsp maple syrup
1 tbsp olive oil
1 tbsp grainy dijon mustard
1 tbsp apple cider vinegar
½ tbsp curry powder
1 tsp minced garlic
1 tsp chilli powder
¼ tsp cumin
½ tsp salt
½ tsp pepper

Directions

Mix all marinade ingredients together and spread over chicken. Marinate for 1 hour minimum or overnight.

Cook in the oven for 20-25 min at 400°F or on the BBQ.

Serves 4

Nutrition Facts

Macronutrients per serving: 190 calories, 23 g protein, 13 g carbs, 4 g fat.

www.cancerfreedomprogram.com

Herb & Tomato Baked

Salmon

Ingredients

1 tbsp olive oil
2 boneless salmon fillet portions
1 tbsp fresh basil
1 tbsp fresh oregano
Salt and pepper, to taste
4 thin slices of tomato
2 tbsp parmesan cheese, grated

Directions

Preheat oven to 375 F. Line baking sheet with parchment paper and brush lightly with some of the olive oil.

Place salmon fillets onto the paper and sprinkle with basil, oregano, salt and pepper. Top with the tomato slices, brush with the rest of the olive oil and add parmesan cheese.

Bake until salmon starts to flake apart when touched and the parmesan is lightly browned (about 15 minutes).

Serves 2

Nutrition Facts

Macronutrients per serving:282 calories, 28 g protein, 3 g carbs, 17 g fat

Shrimp & Pineapple
Skewers

Ingredients

2 cups pineapple chunks
2 tbsp pineapple juice
12 large shrimp, cleaned deveined, tails on
½ tsp garlic salt
Wooden skewers, soaked in water
4 skinless, boneless chicken breasts, cut into 1 ½ inch cubes

Sauce:
2 tsp cornstarch
¼ tsp lemon juice
1 cup orange juice
2 tbsp honey
Dash of pepper

Directions

Thread shrimp, chicken and pineapple on water-soaked wooden skewers, alternating the shrimp and chicken with the pineapple chunks. Place in a shallow dish and sprinkle with pineapple juice. Heat grill to medium.

Place skewers on grill surface and sprinkle with garlic salt. Cook 2-3 minutes per side until shrimp turn pink and chicken is completely cooked through. Remove from grill to a serving platter.

Dissolve cornstarch in lemon juice. In a small saucepan, stir together orange juice, honey and pepper. Bring to boil and stir in cornstarch mixture. Cook 2-3 minutes until thickened. Remove from heat. Serve skewers with dipping sauce. Serves 8

Nutrition Facts

Macronutrients per serving: 120 calories, 14 g protein, 13 g carbs, 1 g fat

Grilled Halibut
with tomato-herb sauce

Ingredients

1 lb halibut fillet
2 tbsp fresh lemon juice
1 tbsp extra virgin olive oil
1 tsp dried, crushed rosemary
½ cup diced tomatoes
¼ cup fresh basil, coarsely chopped
Salt and freshly ground pepper to taste
2 tbsp scallions, finely chopped
1 Tbsp red wine vinegar
1 tsp extra virgin olive oil
½ tsp orange rind, grated
A pinch of cayenne pepper, if desired
Fresh rosemary for garnish, if desired

Directions

Place halibut in a large, shallow dish. In a small bowl, mix together the lemon juice, oil and rosemary for the marinade. Season it with salt and pepper to taste.Pour the marinade over the fish, turning to coat both sides. Cover and refrigerate for at least 30 minutes or up to 4 hours.

Drain the fish and discard the marinade. Place the fish on a greased grill and cook, turning once, until opaque throughout. About 10 mins per inch of thickness.

For the sauce mix together the tomatoes, basil, scallions, vinegar, 1 tsp of oil, orange rind and a pinch of cayenne pepper, if desired. Season with salt and pepper to taste.Heat the sauce on low heat until warm.Garnish grilled fish with some chopped fresh rosemary, if desired, and spoon the sauce over the top. Serve immediately.

Serves 2

Nutrition Facts

Macronutrients per serving:173 calories, 15 g protein, 7 g carbs, 10 g fat

Spicy Broccoli & Tofu

Cancer Recovery Tip:

In the past tofu was thought to increase the risk of cancer recurrence in hormone positive breast cancer. More recently, this has been disproven and has shown to be completely safe.

Ingredients

1 tsp ground cumin
1 tsp ground coriander
2 tbsp canola oil
1 small white onion, cut into small wedges
1 ½ cups broccoli, cut into bite size florets
2 cloves garlic, finely minced
½ tsp chili powder
12 oz extra firm tofu, cut into small cubes
1 cup cauliflower, cut into bite size florets
1 tsp grated fresh ginger

 V

Directions

Heat large, non-stick pan or wok on medium-high heat. Add dry cumin and coriander to pan and dry fry for 1 minute. Stir constantly to avoid burning and sticking. Carefully add oil, garlic and chili powder and stir well to avoid sticking. Stir fry for 2 minutes. Add onion and cook for another 2 minutes. Stir often.

Add the cauliflower and broccoli and cook until hot, but still crisp and brightly colored. Add tofu and toss well until coated with spices and warmed through. Sprinkle with lemon juice.

Serves 4

Nutrition Facts

Macronutrients: 155 calories, 11 g protein, 12 g carbs, 7 g fat.

www.cancerfreedomprogram.com

Grilled Chicken
with Avocado Salsa

Cancer Recovery Tip:
Eating enough protein is key to maintaining and building lean muscle. When coupled with strength training exercises, protein is fundamental in forced menopause weight loss.

Ingredients

Salsa:
4 ripe plum tomatoes, chopped
½ small red onion, finely chopped
1 jalapeno pepper, seeded and diced
2 tbsp fresh cilantro, chopped
¼ cup fresh lime juice, divided
½ avocado, peeled

Chicken:
½ cup plain nonfat yogurt
½ small red onion, coarsely chopped
¼ cup fresh lime juice
¼ cup fresh cilantro
4 boneless, skinless chicken breasts
Salt and pepper

Directions

To make the salsa, combine all ingredients except avocado and lime. Chop avocado and sprinkle with 2 tbsp of lime juice. Add avocado and remaining lime juice into the bowl and toss to combine In a small food processor, puree yogurt, red onion, lime juice and cilantro to make a yogurt marinade. Transfer marinade to a shallow bowl or a plastic bag. Add chicken and coat well. Refrigerate 1 to 8 hours.

Preheat a grill to medium-high heat. Remove chicken from marinade; discard remaining marinade and season chicken with salt and pepper.Grill chicken on both sides until cooked through, about 6 minutes per side. Serve chicken breast with avocado salsa.

Serves 4

Nutrition Facts

Macronutrients: 287 calories, 49 g protein, 11 g carbs, 5 g fat.

www.cancerfreedomprogram.com

Lemon-Soy Baked Tofu
Steaks

Ingredients

12 blocks of firm tofu, sliced into ½-inch thick slices

Marinade:
⅔ cup soy sauce
2 tsp lemon, grated and zested
4 tbsp lemon juice
2 tbsp balsamic vinegar
2 tsp sugar
4 tbsp olive oil
2 cloves garlic, crushed and sliced
2 tbsp chopped fresh thyme

Directions

Lay the tofu out on a board or tray lined with paper towels or a clean tea towel. Cover with more paper. Lay a wooden cutting board or other weight on top to press out the excess moisture. This will take about 30 minutes.

Preheat the oven to 400 °F. Put all the ingredients together in a saucepan, except the herbs. Bring to a boil. Take it off the heat immediately and cool. Add the herbs once the marinade is off the heat.

Once the tofu is drained, pat the slices dry. Spoon a little marinade onto a lightly greased baking dish and lay the tofu slices over it, side by side in a single layer. Pour the rest of the marinade over them. Bake uncovered for 25 minutes, turning the slices over about halfway through. The tofu should be brown and almost dry, and any remaining marinade thick and syrupy.

Serves 8

 V

Nutrition Facts

Macronutrients per serving: 199 calories, 15 g protein, 7 g carbs, 14 g fat

Smoky Tempeh

Ingredients

1 tbsp smoked paprika
2 tbsp lemon juice
1 tbsp maple syrup
½ tsp salt
1 x 8 ounce block of classic pasteurized tempeh

Directions

In a bowl, beat together the smoked paprika, lemon juice, maple syrup and salt. Take the block of tempeh and rub the marinade into it on all sides.

Put the tempeh into a plastic bag along with any remaining marinade and let sit for at least an hour. Overnight is best.

Grill or broil over a medium flame on both sides until well browned and cooked through. Thinly slice and use as you want.

 V

Serves 4

Nutrition Facts

Macronutrients per serving: 129 calories, 11 g protein, 10 g carbs, 6 g fat

Peri Peri Turkey
Kebabs

Ingredients

240 g turkey breast, diced
1 red pepper, deseeded and
cut into 2 cm pieces
12 cherry tomatoes
160 g mixed salad leaves

For the peri-peri marinade:
1-2 red chillies, trimmed
(deseeded for a milder taste)
1 clove garlic, peeled
½ lemon, juice only
1 tsp smoked paprika
1 tbsp rapeseed oil

Directions

Place all the peri-peri
ingredients in a food processor
and blend into a smooth
marinade.

Put the turkey in a bowl and add the peri-peri marinade. Using your hands, mix, coating all sides of the turkey in the marinade. Cover and refrigerate for 1-2 hours for a stronger flavor.

Alternating between turkey, pepper and cherry tomatoes, assemble the kebabs on skewers.

Turn the grill on to high.

Transfer the kebabs onto a foil-lined baking tray and cook under the grill for 15-20 minutes, turning occasionally, until the turkey is cooked through.

Serves: 2

Nutrition Facts
Macronutrients per serving: 265 calories, 34 g protein, 14 g carbs, 8 g fat

Roasted Cauliflower
with Spiced Tomatoes

Cancer Recovery Tip:
Taste changes are unfortunately normal after cancer treatment. Adding flavourful seasonings and spices such as cumin, coriander, cardamom is a great way to solve unpleasant tastes.

Ingredients

1 tsp ground cumin
½ tsp ground coriander
¼ tsp ground cardamom
⅛ tsp ground pepper, preferably white
2 tbsp canola oil, divided
7-8 cups medium cauliflower florets
1 tbsp garlic, finely chopped
1 can (8 oz.) tomato sauce
2 tbsp tomato paste
2 tsp raw sugar
2 tsp white distilled vinegar
⅛ tsp ground cloves
⅛-¼ tsp ground cayenne pepper
½ tsp salt

 V

Directions

In a large mixing bowl, combine cumin, coriander, cardamom, ground pepper and 1 tbsp oil. Add cauliflower, toss and rub to coat.

Line 11-inch x 15-inch jelly roll pan with foil. Coat foil with cooking spray. Arrange cauliflower in one layer. Bake for 10 minutes. Stir, then bake 10 more minutes.

Meanwhile, in a small saucepan, heat remaining oil over medium-high heat. Add garlic and cook, stirring, until fragrant, 1 minute. Add tomato sauce, tomato paste, sugar, vinegar, cloves, cayenne and salt and mix to combine. Cook until the sauce bubbles vigorously around the edges of the pot.

Spoon tomato sauce over cauliflower and mix with spatula until well coated. Roast for 10 minutes. Serve hot or warm.

Serves 2

Nutrition Facts

Macronutrients per serving: 100 calories, 3 g protein, 13 g carbs, 5 g fat

www.cancerfreedomprogram.com

Honey Sriracha Chicken

Ingredients

½ cup plus 2 tablespoons sriracha sauce, divided
2 tbsp honey
6 boneless skinless chicken thighs (about 2 pounds)
3 tbsp lime juice
3 tbsp fresh cilantro, chopped

Directions

In small bowl, mix together 2 tbsp sriracha sauce and place chicken in a resealable plastic bag. Add remaining sriracha sauce and lime juice to chicken. Coat chicken in bag and let stand 15 minutes.

Spray grill grates with nonstick cooking spray and preheat to medium. Place chicken on grill and sear on medium high on both sides. Continue cooking on indirect heat for around 15-20 minutes or until the chicken is done.

Transfer chicken to a platter, brush with reserved sriracha-honey sauce mixture, cover, let stand for 5 minutes. Sprinkle with cilantro.

Serves 6

Nutrition Facts

Macronutrients per serving: 216 calories, 29 g protein, 9 g carbs, 6 g fat

Sweet Potatoe Chili

Ingredients

4 cups sweet potato, 2 inch chunks
1 onion, chopped
1 tsp garlic, minced
1 (15-ounce) can dark red kidney beans, rinsed and drained
1 red bell pepper, cored and chopped
1 (14 ½ ounce) can fire roasted diced tomatoes
2 tbsp chili powder

1 tsp ground cumin
1 ½ tsp paprika
1 cup vegetable broth
½ cup water

Directions

Add all ingredients to a 6-quart slow cooker. Cook on LOW 6-8 hours, or until sweet potatoes are tender. Serve.

Serves 8

 V

Nutrition Facts

Macronutrients per serving: 166 calories, 6 g protein, 37 g carbs, 1 g fat

Eggplant & Beef
Bake

Ingredients

6 cups eggplant, peeled and
chopped
1 onion, chopped
1 tsp garlic, minced
½ pound ground sirloin
1 tsp dried oregano leaves
½ tsp dried basil leaves
3 cups cooked rice
salt and pepper to taste
2 cups marinara sauce

Directions

Preheat oven to 350°F

In a large nonstick skillet coated with nonstick
cooking spray, sauté eggplant, onion, garlic,
and meat until meat is done and eggplant is
tender, about 20 minutes. Add oregano, basil,
and rice. Season to taste and mix well.

Transfer to a 2-quart casserole dish. Cover with
marinara sauce and sprinkle with cheese. Bake
for 20-30 minutes or until thoroughly heated.

Serves 8

Nutrition Facts

Macronutrients per serving:212 calories, 13 g protein, 28 g carbs, 6 g fat

Creamed Spinach

Ingredients

2 tbsp olive oil
1 shallot, minced
1 garlic clove, minced
2 tbsp flour
1 ½ cups low fat milk
2 x 10 oz boxes of frozen
spinach, thawed and drained
¼ cup parmesan cheese,
grated
¼ cup low fat cream cheese
Salt, to taste
Pepper, to taste

Directions

Heat oil in large sauté pan and cook
shallot and garlic until softened. About 3
minutes. Sprinkle flour over mixture and
cook until golden brown. Whisk in milk and
cook until thick and bubbly.

Turn heat to low and stir in both cheeses
until all are incorporated. Gently fold in
spinach and heat until warmed. Season
with salt and pepper.

Serves 4

Nutrition Facts

Macronutrients per serving: 234 calories, 11 g protein, 18 g carbs, 12 g fat.

Miso Chicken & Tzatziki
Wraps

Ingredients
14 small boneless chicken thighs
1 tsp miso paste
1 tsp smoked paprika
1 tsp mixed herbs
2 tsp garlic paste
3 tbsp pickle brine
Ground black pepper, to taste
¼ fresh cucumber
Jar of pickled cucumbers
Small handful of mint, finely chopped
Handful of dill, finely chopped
4 tbsp low-fat yogurt
Spray oil

To serve:
2 Greek-style flatbread or wholemeal tortilla wraps
Mint leaves, Dill leaves, Pickles

Directions
Cut the chicken into small strips and place into a mixing bowl. Add the miso paste, smoked paprika, mixed herbs, and 1 tsp of the garlic paste. Add the pickle brine, season with black pepper, and mix well. Marinate for at least 45 minutes.

For the Tzatziki, dice the fresh cucumber and 3 pickled cucumbers. Add the chopped herbs, and mix in yogurt. Add in 1 tsp of garlic paste and stir well. This can be kept in the fridge for up to 2 days.

On medium-high heat, cook chicken on the grill all the way through.

To serve, warm the flatbreads on the grill for 1-2 minutes. Spoon over tzatziki and add the chicken. Finish with fresh herbs and pickles, and serve.

Serves 2

Nutrition Facts
Macronutrients per serving:262 calories, 20 g protein, 24 g carbs, 11 g fat

Piccalilli Chicken

Ingredients

1 onion, halved
1 head cauliflower, florets removed
3 tsp cornstarch
3 tsp wholegrain mustard
1 green chilli
1 tsp mustard powder
1 tsp turmeric
1 tsp coriander seeds
100 mL sherry vinegar
3 tsp maple syrup
2 bay leaves
2 medium chicken breasts sliced into 6 strips
180 g broccol

Directions

Preheat the oven to 400 F
Place onion and cauliflower on a large baking tray. Spray with oil and place into the oven for 15-20 minutes until the onion is beginning to soften and the cauliflower is lightly golden.

Meanwhile, boil the kettle. In a jug, mix together the remaining ingredients, except for the chicken and broccoli. Add roughly 100 mL the of freshly boiled water, and stir well. The mixture should be mustard yellow and glossy.

After 15 minutes, add the chicken to the baking tray on top of the onion and cauliflower, and pour the sauce over the chicken, coating the onion and cauliflower. Add a couple sprays of oil to the chicken and then place the tray back into the oven for 20 minutes.

After 20 minutes, carefully remove the tray from the oven and spoon the thickened sauce over the chicken and vegetables to glaze. Add in the broccoli and pop back into the oven for a further 15 minutes. Once the chicken is cooked, leave it to rest for 5 minutes to allow the meat to become tender.

Serves 2

Nutrition Facts

Macronutrients per serving:340 calories, 37 g protein, 41 g carbs, 5 g fat

Slow Cooker Quinoa
Risotto

Cancer Recovery Tip:
Quinoa is an excellent source of protein and fibre. Both are critical in your cancer recovery.

Ingredients

1 ½ cups quinoa, uncooked and rinsed
1 ½ lbs skinless, boneless chicken breasts, cut into bite-size pieces
3 cups mushrooms, sliced
3 cups low-sodium chicken broth
1 large shallot, thinly sliced
5 cloves garlic, minced
½ tsp each of dried thyme, basil and oregano
1 tbsp coconut oil
½ tsp pepper
Juice of 1 lemon
4 cups spinach, roughly chopped, packed
⅔ cup parmesan cheese, grated

Directions

Place all ingredients except spinach and cheese in slow cooker.

Cover and cook on low for 3 hours.

When almost done cooking, the liquid should be absorbed, and the mixture should be slightly sticky. Stir in spinach and cheese, cover and continue cooking just until spinach begins to wilt (about 2-5 minutes).

Serves 6

Nutrition Facts
Macronutrients per serving: 380 calories, 37 g protein, 32 g carbs, 11 g fat.

www.cancerfreedomprogram.com

Stuffed Peppers
With Turkey & Wild Rice

Ingredients

1 tbsp olive oil
½ medium onion, chopped
1 cup coarsely chopped mushrooms
1 lb ground turkey
2 cups baby spinach leaves, chopped
1 cup tomatoes, diced
2 cloves garlic, minced
1 tsp paprika
1 tsp oregano
¾ cup carrots, steamed and cut into ½ -inch chunks
1 ½ cups wild rice, cooked
4 large green or red bell peppers, tops removed and seeded (save tops to cover peppers during baking for a moister filling)
Salt and pepper, to taste

Directions

Preheat oven to 350 F

In a skillet over medium-high heat, heat oil. Sauté onion and mushrooms until onions are translucent. Add turkey, spinach, tomatoes, garlic and seasonings and cook until turkey is cooked through, about 5-6 minutes.

Place turkey mixture in large mixing bowl and add carrots and wild rice. Combine well. Using spoon, lightly pack mixture into peppers.

Place peppers in 9-inch square oven dish, add 1/4 cup water to bottom of pan and bake about 45-50 minutes or until peppers are just tender. Serve.

Serves 4

Nutrition Facts

Macronutrients per serving:330 calories, 28 g protein, 27 g carbs, 13 g fat

Cancer Recovery Tip:

Focus on incorporating a lean protein source at every meal.

Turkey Meatloaf

Ingredients

1 tsp olive oil
1 small onion, chopped
2-3 cloves of garlic, finely chopped
1 tsp dried greek oregano
2-3 tbsp Dijon mustard
½ tsp black pepper
¼ to ½ tsp salt
¾ cup tomato ketchup
½ cup fresh italian flat-leaf parsley leaves, chopped
2 slices bread
½ cup chicken stock
1 large egg, lightly beaten
2 lbs lean ground chicken or turkey

Directions

Preheat oven to 350 F. Lightly grease an 8x4 inch loaf pan. Place a medium-sized skillet over low heat and when it is hot, add oil. Add onion, garlic and oregano, cook until the onion is golden, about 10 minutes. Transfer to a large mixing bowl and set aside to cool.

In the meantime, soak the bread in the stock until it is moist, about 2 minutes. Drain off as much liquid as possible. Add the bread to the cooled onion mixture. Add the eggs and ground meat and mix by hand until everything is thoroughly incorporated. Place the mixture into the prepared loaf pan, transfer into the oven and cook for about 1 hour and 15 minutes.

Serves 10

Nutrition Facts

Macronutrients per serving: 162 calories, 14 g protein, 8 g carbs, 8 g fat

www.cancerfreedomprogram.com

Paprika Shrimp
With Walnuts

Ingredients

2 tbsp canola oil
1 tbsp fresh ginger, minced
1 ½ tsp paprika
3 tbsp walnuts, chopped
20 large shrimp, peeled and deveined
1 ½ cups turnips, washed, peeled, and cubed
1 tbsp cider vinegar
3 tbsp rice wine
¼ cup fresh parsley
Salt and pepper to taste

Directions

Heat oil in a skillet over medium heat, add ginger and paprika and cook until fragrant, about 30 seconds. Add walnuts and sauté until lightly browned, 2-3 minutes.

Add shrimp and cook, stirring occasionally, until pink, about 2 minutes per side. Stir in turnips, vinegar and rice wine and season with salt and pepper. Continue cooking until heated through, about 2 minutes. Top with parsley and serve.

Serves 4

Nutrition Facts

Macronutrients per serving:304 calories, 37 g protein, 9 g carbs, 12 g fat

Chicken Salad
With 3-Citrus Dressing

Ingredients

1 pound skinless and boneless chicken breast
2 garlic cloves, chopped
Salt to taste
¾ cup orange juice
2 tbsp fresh lime juice
1 tbsp lemon juice
1 tsp ground cumin
1 tbsp honey mustard
Ground black pepper
2 tbsp extra-virgin olive oil, divided
8 packed cups spinach leaves, washed and stemmed
1 (11 ounce) can mandarin orange sections, drained

Directions

Cut chicken lengthwise into 1-inch strips and place in a resealable plastic bag.

Place chopped garlic in a small bowl and add a pinch of salt, mash together to create a paste. Add orange juice, lime and lemon juices, cumin, honey mustard and black pepper to taste. Whisk in one tbsp of oil.

Pour 1/2 cup of dressing into the bag with chicken, massage to coat chicken strips. Marinate chicken in the refrigerator for 1-2 hours. Discard marinade.

Cook chicken in a heated pan on medium-high heat until pieces are white at thickest point, turn them over often to prevent charring. Transfer to a plate and let chicken rest for five minutes, cut into one-inch pieces.

In a large bowl combine spinach and chicken. Whisk remaining one tbsp of oil with dressing and pour over spinach and chicken. Toss to combine. Top with mandarin oranges and walnuts and serve.
Serves: 2

Nutrition Facts

Macronutrients per serving:212 calories, 16 g protein, 7 g carbs, 15 g fat

Snacks

Dorito Roasted Chickpeas

Ingredients

1 can chickpeas
3 tbsp nutritional yeast
½ tsp garlic powder
½ tsp onion flashes
⅛ tsp dried mustard
¼ tsp dried parsley
¼ tsp sea salt
¼ tsp black pepper

Directions

Drain and rinse canned chickpeas. Line the baking sheet with tin foil and spread chickpeas evenly. Roast in the oven at 425 F for 25 minutes. While roasting, mix all remaining ingredients.

Remove chickpeas from the oven and toss in seasoning immediately.

Serves 6

 V

Nutrition Facts

Macronutrients per serving:90 calories, 4 g protein, 11 g carbs, 3 g fat

Healthy Deviled Eggs

Ingredients

6 large eggs
3 tbsp 0% greek yogurt
1 tsp dijon mustard
1 tsp lemon juice
Optional garnish: Paprika

Directions

Put eggs in a pot and add cold water until the eggs are submerged. Cover and bring to a boil over high heat. Once boiling, remove pot from heat and let sit for 10 min.

Fill a large bowl with cold water and ice cubes. Once eggs have sat for 10 min, remove them from the hot water and place in ice bath until cooled completely. Peel eggs, rinse, and cut lengthwise. Gently remove yolk.

Mash yolks with a fork and stir in greek yogurt, mustard, and lemon juice. Spoon mixture back into egg whites and garnish as desired. Enjoy.

Serving size: 2 halves

Nutrition Facts

Macronutrients per serving:82 calories, 7 g protein, 1 g carbs, 2 g fat

Healthy Blueberry
Muffins

Ingredients

Non-stick cooking spray
1 cup whole wheat flour
¾ cup all purpose flour
½ cup firmly packed light brown sugar
1 tbsp + 1tsp baking powder
1 tsp ground cinnamon
½ tsp ground allspice
½ tsp salt
1 cup nonfat yogurt
2 tbsp canola oil
2 tbsp unsweetened applesauce
1 egg lightly beaten
1 cup fresh or frozen blueberries

Directions

Preheat the oven to 400 F. Lightly spray a muffin tin with cooking spray.

In a large bowl, combine the flours, brown sugar, baking powder, cinnamon, allspice and salt. In another bowl, whisk together the yogurt, applesauce and egg. Pour the wet mixture into the dry mixture, stirring until it is just combined (do not over mix). Lightly stir in the blueberries.

Spoon the batter evenly into the prepared muffin cups. Bake until the tops are golden, 20-25 minutes. Serve warm.

Serves 12 muffins

Nutrition Facts

Macronutrients per serving: 112 calories, 3 g protein, 19 g carbs, 3 g fat.

www.cancerfreedomprogram.com

Banana Chocolate Chip
Muffins

Ingredients

6 mashed bananas
½ cup 0% greek yogurt
½ cup egg whites
½ cup brown sugar
2 tsp baking soda
Dash salt
½ tsp vanilla extract
3 cup all purpose flour
⅓ cup chocolate chips

Directions

Mash bananas in a medium mixing bowl.
Add all ingredients (except flour and
chocolate chips). Mix until all dry
ingredients are wet. Gradually mix in
flour. Stir in chocolate chips.

Spray muffin tin with non-stick spray.
Separate equally into 24 muffins. Cook at
350°F for 20-30 min.

Serves 24 muffins

Nutrition Facts

Macronutrients per serving: 118 calories, 3 g protein, 24 g carbs, 1 g fat

Black Bean
Brownies

Ingredients

1 ¼ cup canned black beans,
rinsed and drained
½ cup egg whites
½ cup chocolate protein
powder
¼ cup low fat cottage cheese
½ cup cocoa powder
6 tbsp Calorie free syrup
3 tbsp coconut flour
1 tsp baking powder

Directions

Using an immersion blender or food processor,
blend all ingredients together and place in a
9X9 cake pan.

Bake for 40-45 min or until a knife inserted into
the middle comes out clean. Cook until ideally a
bit gooey in the center.

Let cool and remove from the pan. Sprinkle a bit
of cocoa on top.Divide into 8 pieces.
Serve with low fat ice cream or your favorite
fruit on top.

Serves 8 brownies

Nutrition Facts

Macronutrients per serving:155 calories, 13 g protein, 19 g carbs, 2.5 g fat

Melon Salad

Ingredients

1 lb watermelon
½ lb honeydew melon
½ lb cantaloupe
4 tbsp low fat feta cheese, diced
2 tbsp mint leaves, finely chopped
Juice of 1 lime
Salt & pepper to taste, if desired
Whole sprigs of mint leaves for garnish
(optional)

Directions

Seed the melons and cut into bite-sized pieces.
Arrange them on a platter. Sprinkle with the feta
cheese and chopped mint. Season with lime
juice and, if desired, a pinch of salt and pepper
to taste. If using, garnish with sprigs of mint.

Serves 6

Nutrition Facts

Macronutrients per serving:69 calories, 2 g protein, 13 g carbs, 2 g fat

Watermelon & Mint
Salad

Ingredients

6 cup watermelon, cubed
1 cup low-fat feta cheese, cubed
¼ cup red onion, chopped
¼ cup fresh mint, chopped
2 Tbsp olive oil
1 lime, juice and zest
Salt and pepper to taste

Directions

Add the watermelon to a large bowl with the red onion. Gently toss to combine. Add the feta and mint. Drizzle with olive oil and season with salt and pepper.

Serves 6

Nutrition Facts

Macronutrients per serving: 160 calories, 5 g protein, 15 g carbs, 10 g fat

Cancer Recovery Tip:

Dips are a great way to help you meet your calorie goals if you struggle with a low appetite.

White Bean
Dip

Ingredients

¼ cup assorted fresh herbs such as parsley, basil, cilantro, and/or mint leaves
2 garlic cloves
1 16 oz. can white beans, drained and rinsed
2 tbsp nonfat greek yogurt
Juice from ½ of a lemon
¼ tsp kosher salt

Directions

Chop the herbs and garlic in a food processor. Add the remaining ingredients and process until smooth. Cover and refrigerate for at least 1 hour.

Serves 20 (1 serving= 1 tbsp)

Nutrition Facts

Macronutrients per serving:76 calories, 6 g protein, 14 g carbs, 0 g fat

Banana Peach
Sorbet

Ingredients

2 overripe bananas, thinly
sliced and frozen
2 cups chopped fresh peaches,
peeled if desired and frozen
½ tsp vanilla extract
⅓ cup plain, low-fat yogurt

Directions

Place the frozen bananas and peaches in the
bowl of a food processor and blend until
smooth. Gradually add the vanilla and yogurt
and process until completely incorporated.
Serve immediately.

Serves 4

Nutrition Facts

Macronutrients per serving:93 calories, 14 g protein, 22 g carbs, 1 g fat

Rhubarb Strawberry
Compote

Ingredients

4 cups washed, trimmed and
chopped rhubarb stalks,
remove and discard the leaves
3 cups chopped strawberries
1 tsp cornstarch
1 tbsp brown sugar
1 tsp lemon zest

Directions

Place the rhubarb, berries and cornstarch in a
medium saucepan and cook over medium heat
until it reaches a low boil, about 7 minutes.
Lower the heat to low and cook until the
rhubarb is soft and the mixture has thickened,
about 30 minutes.

Remove from heat and add the sugar and lemon
zest. Serve room or at room temperature.

 V

Serves 4

Nutrition Facts

Macronutrients per serving: 73 calories, 2 g protein, 17 g carbs, 1 g fat

Buffalo Cauliflower
Bites

Ingredients

Cooking spray
2 medium heads cauliflower, cut into small florets
1 cup all purpose flour
1 cup water
2 tsp garlic powder
1 tsp salt
2 tsp butter
1 ⅓ cups hot sauce

Directions

Preheat the oven to 450 F. Spray a baking sheet with cooking spray.

Toss the cauliflower florets with flour, water, garlic powder, and salt. Place on the prepared baking sheet and bake for 20 minutes.
In a small saucepan, melt butter with hot sauce. Pour butter mixture over baked cauliflower and toss to coat.
Return cauliflower to the oven and bake for another 20 minutes. Serve warm.

Serves 4

V

Nutrition Facts
Macronutrients per serving: 130 calories, 7 g protein, 20 g carbs, 3 g fat

Maple Pear Brulee
with Coconut Yogurt

Ingredients

2 pears, peeled, cored and sliced lengthways
1 tbsp maple syrup
15 g currants
1 lemon, zest and juice
100 g fat-free coconut-flavored yogurt

Directions

Preheat the oven to 350 F.

Place the pears on a baking tray, brush with the maple syrup and bake for 20-25 minutes, until they are just browning at the edges. Set aside and leave to cool slightly.

Meanwhile, pour the lemon juice into a small bowl and add the currants. Allow to soak to plump up.

Divide the yogurt equally between two bowls and top each with a whole pear. Sprinkle over the lemony currants and serve.

Serves 2

Nutrition Facts

Macronutrients per serving: 107 calories, 3 g protein, 23 g carbs, 0 g fat

Pumpkin Oatmeal
Bars

Ingredients

2 cups all purpose flour
⅓ cups rolled oats
1 tsp baking soda
¾ tsp salt
1 tsp cinnamon
½ tsp nutmeg
1 ⅓ cup sugar
⅔ cup canola oil
3 tbsp molasses
1 can of cooked pumpkin puree
1 tsp vanilla
2 tbsp ground flaxseed

Directions

Preheat the oven to 350 F. Spray two 12 x 17 baking sheet pans with non-stick cooking spray.

Mix together flour, oats, baking soda, salt, and spices.In a separate bowl, mix together sugar, oil, molasses, pumpkin, vanilla, and optional flax seeds until combined.

Mix flour and sugar mixtures together.

Spread and press batter onto greased cookie sheets. Bake for 16 minutes or until a inserted toothpick is clean.

Remove from the oven. Once cool, slice into 20 bars per sheet pan.

Serves 40 bars

 V

Nutrition Facts

Macronutrients per serving: 101 calories, 1 g protein, 15 g carbs, 4 g fat

www.cancerfreedomprogram.com

Maple Walnut
Granola

Ingredients

Nonstick cooking spray
3 cups oats
¼ cup all purpose flour
¼ cup chopped english walnuts
½ tsp cinnamon
Pinch of salt
⅓ cup maple syrup
⅓ cup canola oil
1 tsp vanilla extract

Directions

Preheat the oven to 300 F. Lightly coat a large baking sheet with cooking spray.

In a large bowl, combine oats, flour, walnuts, cinnamon and salt. In a separate bowl whisk together maple syrup, oil and vanilla. Add to oat mixture, stirring well.

On a large baking sheet, evenly spread the mixture and bake for 30 minutes. Remove the tray from the oven and stir granola, breaking up any lumps. Return to the oven and bake for an additional 20 minutes.

Remove from the oven and allow granola to cool completely. Serve.

Serves 10 (1/2 cup per serving)

 V

Nutrition Facts

Macronutrients per serving:220 calories, 4 g protein, 27 g carbs, 11 g fat

Recovery Granola
Bars

Ingredients

¼ cup chopped nuts (any variety)
1 ½ cup oats
2 tbsp butter
2 tbsp sugar
1/8 cup of honey
¼ tsp vanilla
¼ tsp salt
¼ cup dried fruit
2-3 tbsp chocolate chips

Directions

Spray a baking pan with non-stick cooking spray. Add chopped nuts and oatmeal. Mix well.

Bake at 350 F for 5-10 minutes or until browned. Flip halfway through.

In a small saucepan mix together butter, sugar, honey, vanilla and salt. Combine wet and dry ingredients. Mix well. Add in fried fruit and chocolate. Spray a dish with non-stick cooking spray. Transfer mixture and firmly press the mixture into the dish.

Refrigerate for two hours.

Remove the mixture from the dish and cut into eight bars.

Serves 8

Nutrition Facts

Macronutrients per serving: 122 calories, 2 g protein, 17 g carbs, 9 g fat

Cranberry Granola
Crunch

Cancer Recovery Tip:
Fibre is important in helping our bodies stabilize blood sugar levels and can help keep you feeling fuller for longer.

Ingredients

2 cups oats
¼ cup ground flaxseed
½ cup pecans, chopped
½ cup pumpkin seeds
3 tbsp maple syrup
2 tbsp extra virgin olive oil
½ tsp vanilla extract
1 tsp cinnamon
⅓ cup dried cranberries, chopped

 V

Directions

Preheat the oven to 325° F.

Combine all ingredients (except dried fruit) in a mixing bowl. Use your hands to mix well and toss to coat. Spread the mixture in a thin layer on a baking sheet and bake for 20-25 minutes, stirring halfway through.

Mix in the dried fruit once the granola has cooled.

Serves 8

Nutrition Facts

Macronutrients per serving: 280 calories, 14 g protein, 27 g carbs, 16 g fat

Energy Bites

Ingredients

2 cups oats
1 cup pitted dates, chopped
¾ cup pumpkin seeds
¼ cup ground flaxseed
1 tsp cinnamon
¾ cup unsweetened applesauce
½ cup peanut butter
1 ½ tbsp honey
½ cup almonds, crushed

 V

Directions

Line a baking sheet with parchment paper.In a large mixing bowl combine all of the ingredients (except the crushed almonds).

Roll mixture into 1 tbsp balls. Roll the balls in crushed almonds. Place them on a prepared baking sheet.

Refrigerate for at least 3 hours before serving.

Serves 10

Nutrition Facts

Macronutrients per serving:293 calories, 11 g protein, 30 g carbs, 17 g fat

Cancer Recovery Tip:

These energy bites are a quick source of calories if you are struggling with low appetite.

Oatmeal Power
Balls

Ingredients

1 cup oats
½ cup smooth peanut butter
½ cup pecans, chopped
3 tbsp unsweetened cocoa powder
2 tbsp unsweetened shredded coconut (plus
1 tablespoon for rolling at end)
½ tsp cinnamon
1 tsp vanilla extract
½ tsp salt
1 tbsp maple syrup
2 tablespoons unsweetened almond milk

Directions

Combine all ingredients in a large bowl. Using hands, roll mixture into balls (approximately 1 inch in diameter). Roll finished balls in shredded coconut.

Place balls an inch apart in an airtight container to freeze for an hour. Once frozen, refrigerate.

Serves 8

Nutrition Facts

Macronutrients per serving: 180 calories, 6 g protein, 20 g carbs, 10 g fat

Peanut Butter
Energy Bites

Cancer Recovery Tip:
If you are struggling with a low appetite, various nut butters (peanut, almond) is a great way to help you quicky eat the calories you need.

Ingredients

⅔ cup peanut butter
1 cup oats, plus extra for rolling
1½ tbsp honey
¼ cup miniature dark chocolate chips, plus extra for rolling
¼ cup ground flax seed

Directions

Mix all ingredients in a bowl until well-combined. Cover with plastic wrap and chill in the refrigerator for at least 30 minutes.

After 30 minutes, roll into approximately 1 inch balls. Lay out a thin layer of oats and chocolate chips on a cutting board or work surface and roll the balls in the mixture. Finish off by rolling each ball between your hands to pack in the oats and chocolate chips. Store in the refrigerator until ready to be eaten.

Serves 18

Nutrition Facts

Macronutrients per serving:99 calories, 3 g protein, 7 g carbs, 7 g fat

Spiced Roasted
Chickpeas

Ingredients

1 tsp ground cumin
1 tsp smoked sweet paprika
½ tsp garlic powder
½ tsp onion powder
⅛ tsp salt
⅛ tsp black pepper
Pinch of cayenne pepper
2 tbsp extra-virgin olive oil
1 15-ounce can chickpeas,
drained

Directions

Preheat the oven to 400 F.In a
medium mixing bowl, use a
small whisk to combine
cumin, paprika, garlic powder,
onion powder, salt, black
pepper, cayenne. Add oil and
whisk to combine.

Place a double layer of paper towels on a
work surface. Rinse chickpeas in a
colander. Shake well, then spread
chickpeas evenly across paper towels.
Blot chickpeas using a clean paper towel.
Repeat as needed, until chickpeas are
thoroughly dry.

Add chickpeas to spice mixture and,
using your fingers, gently mix and
massage until they are evenly coated.

Line a baking sheet with parchment
paper and spread chickpeas evenly
across the pan.Bake, stirring every 8
minutes, until chickpeas are firm,
approximately 30 minutes.

Remove the sheet from the oven and
allow chickpeas to cool. Serve
immediately or transfer to an airtight
container.

 V

Serves 4

Nutrition Facts

Macronutrients per serving:170 calories, 6 g protein, 20 g carbs, 8 g fat

Healthy Granola
Bars

Ingredients

¼ cup chopped nuts (any variety)
1 ½ cup oats
2 tbsp butter
2 tbsp sugar
1/8 cup of honey
¼ tsp vanilla
¼ tsp salt
¼ cup dried fruit
2-3 tbsp chocolate chips

Directions

Spray a baking pan with non-stick cooking spray. Add chopped nuts and oatmeal. Mix well.

Bake at 350 F for 5-10 minutes or until browned. Flip halfway through.

In a small saucepan mix together butter, sugar, honey, vanilla and salt. Combine wet and dry ingredients. Mix well. Add in fried fruit and chocolate. Spray a dish with non-stick cooking spray. Transfer mixture and firmly press the mixture into the dish.

Refrigerate for two hours.

Remove the mixture from the dish and cut into eight bars.

Serves 8

Nutrition Facts

Macronutrients per serving: 122 calories, 2 g protein, 17 g carbs, 9 g fat

Chocolate Coconut
Bites

Ingredients

½ cup pecans
15 whole pitted dates, roughly chopped
⅓ cup unsweetened shredded coconut
1 tsp coconut oil
1 ½ tbsp cocoa powder
½ tsp salt
1 tbsp water

 V

Directions

Place pecans in a food processor and pulse until roughly chopped. Add remaining ingredients and process until mixture starts to form. Using a tablespoon measure, spoon out mixture and roll into 12 balls. Store in the fridge in an airtight container for up to two weeks, or in the freezer for up to 3 months.

Serves 12

Nutrition Facts

Macronutrients per serving: 126 calories, 1 g protein, 23 g carbs, 4 g fat

Lemon Poppyseed
Muffin

Ingredients

1 cup plain, non-fat greek yogurt
¼ cup avocado oil
Juice of 1 lemon
1 egg
½ cup maple syrup
1 tsp vanilla extract
1 ¾ cup all-purpose flour
¾ tbsp poppy seeds
Zest of 1 lemon
1 tsp baking soda
¼ tsp salt
1 cup frozen blueberries

Directions

Line a 12 cup muffin tin with liners. In a large bowl, mix the yogurt, oil, lemon juice, egg, maple syrup and vanilla extract together until combined. Add the flour, poppy seeds, lemon zest, baking soda and salt to the liquid mixture and stir until just combined. Gently fold the blueberries into the batter. Divide the batter evenly between the 12 muffin cups.

Bake the muffins for 5 minutes at 425°F, then reduce the heat to 375°F and bake for 15 minutes or until a toothpick inserted comes out clean.

Serves 12

Nutrition Facts

Macronutrients per serving: 172 calories, 4 g protein, 24 g carbs, 6 g fat

www.cancerfreedomprogram.com

Chocolate & Coconut Protein
Donut

Cancer Recovery Tip:
Protein powder can be an easy and convenient way to help you meet your daily protein target.

Ingredients

¼ cup chocolate whey protein powder
¼ cup coconut flour
¼ cup cocoa powder
¼ tsp baking soda
½ tsp baking powder
¼ tsp salk
½ tbsp butter, melted
¼ cup unsweetened applesauce
¼ cup nonfat plain greek or icelandic style yogurt
1 egg
1 tsp vanilla

Cream Cheese Glaze
1 tbsp low-fat cream cheese
12 tsp low-fat milk

Directions

Preheat oven to 350°F. Spray donut pan with non-stick spray.

Mix all dry ingredients together in a large mixing bowl. In a smaller bowl, combine wet ingredients and whisk together. Add wet ingredients to the dry and whisk together until well incorporated.

Transfer batter to a large Ziploc bag. Snip a very small hole in one of the bottom corners of the bag and evenly pipe batter into donut pan.

Bake donuts in the oven for 10 minutes.While donuts are cooling, prepare the glaze. Combine cream cheese and milk in a small flat bowl which is wide enough to dip an entire donut in. Carefully pick up each of the donuts and dunk the tops into the glaze for a light coating. Serve.
Serves: 6

Nutrition Facts

Macronutrients per serving:115 calories, 9 g protein, 8 g carbs, 5.5 g fat

Chocolate Tofu
Mousse

Ingredients

1 package (300 g) soft tofu
2½ tbsp maple syrup
1 tbsp cocoa powder
1 tbsp cornstarch

Directions

Combine soft tofu, maple syrup, cocoa powder and corn starch in blender. Blend until you obtain a smooth consistency.

Divide in four individual bowls and place in the refrigerator for at least 2 hours before serving. Top with fresh berries, shaved chocolate and pumpkin seeds.

Serves 4

 V

Nutrition Facts

Macronutrients per serving:83 calories, 3 g protein, 12 g carbs, 2 g fat

Berry Nut Bark

Ingredients

2 cups plain, non-fat Greek yogurt
2 tbsp honey
1 tsp vanilla extract
⅓ cup pistachios
⅓ cup unsweetened dried cranberries, chopped

Directions

Line a 9 x 13 baking pan with a piece of parchment paper (with overhang) so the bark is easy to remove once frozen.

In a medium mixing bowl, add the yogurt, honey and vanilla and stir well. Spread the yogurt mixture onto the parchment paper-lined baking pan. Sprinkle the top of the yogurt with pistachios and chopped dried cranberries and any other topping of choice.

Freeze for at least 3 hours. Before serving, break up the bark into pieces with a sharp knife.
Let stand at room temperature for about 5-10 minutes before serving.

Serves 10

Nutrition Facts

Macronutrients per serving:63 calories, 4 g protein, 6 g carbs, 3 g fat

Vegan Protein
Crackers

Ingredients

½ cup water
3 Tbsp ground flax seeds
½ cup unsweetened protein powder
½ cup unsweetened shredded coconut
3 Tbsp sesame seeds
1 Tbsp chia seeds
¼ tsp salt
1 Tbsp coconut oil, melted

Directions

Preheat the oven to 300F. Line an 11x8 inch baking sheet with parchment paper and coat it lightly with cooking spray

Combine the water and ground flax seeds in a small bowl. Mix well and set aside

In a separate bowl, combine the protein powder, shredded coconut, sesame and chia seeds, and salt and mix well, Add the melted coconut oil and flax mixture and mix well until all the ingredients are well incorporated

Grease your hands lightly and spread the cracker mixture on the parchment paper as evenly as possible (the mixture will be sticky, so grease your hands again if you need to). You can score the dough using a sharp knife if you want even-sized crackers. Bake for 1 hour

Keeping the oven on, remove the tray and flip the crackers onto the tray. bake for another 15 minutes. Let them cool completely before breaking them

Serves 44 crackers

 V

Nutrition Facts
Macronutrients per serving:22 calories, 1 g protein, 1 g carbs, 11 g fat

Chocolate Zucchini
Bread

Ingredients

1 medium zucchini, shredded
1 cup all-purpose flour
⅓ cup unsweetened cocoa powder
¾ tsp baking soda
¼ tsp baking powder
¼ cup avocado oil
⅓ cup plain, non-fat Greek yogurt
2 eggs
½ cup honey
1 tsp vanilla extract
⅔ cup dark chocolate chips

Directions

Preheat the oven to 350°F. Spray an 8 ½ x 4 ½-inch loaf pan with non-stick cooking spray.

Place shredded zucchini on a clean dish towel or some paper towels to absorb some of the liquid. Set aside.

In a large bowl, whisk together the flour, cocoa powder, baking soda and baking powder.

In a separate medium-sized bowl, whisk the oil, yogurt, eggs, honey and vanilla together until combined.

Pour the wet mixture into the dry mixture and stir until combined. Fold in the shredded zucchini and chocolate chips.

Pour batter into the prepared loaf pan and bake for 30-35 minutes or until a toothpick inserted comes out clean. Cool bread completely in a pan on a wire rack.

Serves 10

Nutrition Facts

Macronutrients per serving:227 calories, 5 g protein, 30 g carbs, 11 g fat

Easy Tofu
Nuggets

Ingredients

16 oz block extra-firm tofu
½ cup unsweetened almond milk
1½ Tbsp cornstarch
1 ½ Tbsp ground flaxseed
¼ tsp salt

1 cup panko breadcrumbs
½ tsp garlic powder
½ tsp smoked paprika
¼ tsp salt

Directions

Wrap the block of tofu in paper towels. Place a plate on top of the wrapped tofu, and put a couple of heavy books on top of that. Press tofu for 20 minutes

In a small bowl, add almond milk, cornstarch, ground flaxseeds and 1/4 teaspoon salt. Whisk and then set aside until the tofu is ready.

Preheat the oven to 400 F and line a large baking sheet with parchment paper.

In another small bowl, combine the breadcrumbs, garlic powder, smoked paprika and 1/4 teaspoon salt. Set aside.

Slice the pressed tofu into equal sized cubes. Coat each tofu cube in the wet ingredients, then into the breadcrumb mixture. Pat with the breadcrumb mixture to get as much as possible on the tofu. Place on the prepared baking sheet with parchment paper.Bake for 15 minutes, then flip the pieces and bake for 15 more minutes, until golden and crispy.

V

Serves 3

Nutrition Facts

Macronutrients per serving:248 calories, 17 g protein, 23 g carbs, 10 g fat

Pumpkin Oatmeal
Cookies

Ingredients

¾ cup oats
½ cup oat flour
¼ tsp salt
¼ tsp baking soda
¼ cup sugar
¼ tsp cinnamon
⅓ cup canned pumpkin
2 to 2 ½ tablespoons milk
1 tbsp oil
½ tsp pure vanilla extract

 V

Directions

Combine all dry ingredients and stir very well.

In a separate bowl, combine all liquid (including pumpkin). Then stir to combine, and form into balls or cookies.

Serves 20

Nutrition Facts

Macronutrients per serving:60 calories, 1 g protein, 10 g carbs, 2 g fat

Sweet Potato & Cranberry Cookies

Ingredients

1 medium sweet potato, baked and mashed
2 tbsp ground flax seed
¼ cup skim milk
¼ cup canola oil
1 tbsp vanilla extract
½ cup brown sugar
2 cups all purpose flour
¾ tsp cinnamon
1 tsp baking soda
½ tsp salt
1 cup oats
½ cup almonds, slivered
¾ cup dried cranberries

Directions

Heat oven to 450 F.

Wash sweet potatoes and pierce with a fork. Bake them for about an hour. Cool then slice sweet potatoes in half and scoop flesh into a large bowl and mash.

Preheat the oven to 350 F and spray baking sheets with non-stick cooking spray.

In a large bowl, combine sweet potato puree, ground flax seed, milk, oil, vanilla and brown sugar. Sift flour, spices, baking soda, and salt and stir until incorporated. Fold in oats, almonds, and dried cranberries. Scoop onto a baking sheet and bake for 12-15 minutes.

Serves 20

Nutrition Facts

Macronutrients per serving: 212 calories, 16 g protein, 7 g carbs, 15 g fat

Marinated Mushrooms

Ingredients

1 lb small button mushrooms, fresh
⅓ cup red wine vinegar
⅓ cup olive oil
1 small white onion, sliced thinly
½ tsp onion salt
¼ tsp celery salt
¼ tsp marjoram
1 clove garlic, minced
2 Tbsp parsley flakes
1 Tbsp brown sugar

 V

Directions

Bring a medium pot of water to a boil. Place the mushrooms into the water and cook for 6-7 minutes. Drain.

Whisk together the marinade ingredients.

Marinate the mushrooms in the mixture in a closed container in the fridge for at least 4 hours, stirring the mixture occasionally to coat the mushrooms. Serve.

Serves 8

Nutrition Facts

Macronutrients per serving: 105 calories, 2 g protein, 5 g carbs, 9 g fat

Cheesy Cauliflower
Tots

Ingredients

1 head cauliflower, washed and trimmed
1 egg
1 egg white
½ cup reduced fat, shredded cheddar
cheese
⅓ cup breadcrumbs
2 scallions (white and green parts), washed,
minced
½ tsp salt
¼ tsp ground black pepper

Directions

Preheat the oven to 400 F. Coat one large
baking sheet with non-stick cooking spray.

Place the cauliflower in the oven for about 10-
12 minutes or until soft. Let it cool, then mince
the cauliflower and place in a large bowl. Stir
the remaining ingredients into the minced
cauliflower and let the mixture stand for 10
minutes. After setting, stir the mixture again.
Using a tablespoon, scoop cauliflower mixture
onto the baking sheet and form into balls.
Repeat to make 35 tots.

Spray each tot with cooking spray. Bake for 15
minutes. Turn the tots and bake for an
additional 10 minutes or until golden brown.
Serve.

Serves 7 (one serving = 5 tater tots)

Nutrition Facts
Macronutrients per serving:65 calories, 4 g protein, 10 g carbs, 2 g fat

www.cancerfreedomprogram.com

Recipes For Your Recovery

Weight Loss

- Open Faced Egg Sandwich
- Spring Vegetable Frittata
- Copy Cat Egg Bites
- Savory Cottage cheese bowl
- Beet and Toasted Pumpkin seed salad
- No mayo tuna salad
- Peri Peri Turkey Kebabs
- Black bean brownies
- Watermelon and mint salad
- Marinated mushrooms

For Low Appetite:

- Chocolate and Chia Seed Overnight Oats
- Peanut Butter Smoothie
- Copy Cat Egg Bites
- Egg and Avocado Toast
- Chicken Orzo Salad
- Hawaiian Start Soup
- Energy bites
- Oatmeal power balls
- Peanut butter energy bites
- Berry Nut Bark
- Easy tofu nuggets
- Cheesy cauliflower tots

Rebuild Energy

- Chocolate and Chia Seed Overnight Oats
- Swiss Chard Frittata
- Greek chicken meatballs
- Meatballs & Zucchini noodles
- Herb and tomato baked salmon
- Grilled chicken with avocado salsa
- Peri Peri Turkey Kebabs
- Turkey Meatloaf
- Healthy Deviled Eggs
- Sweet potato and cranberry cookies

Taste Changes

- Lemon and Chia Seed Parfaits
- Blueberry Crumble
- Peach Ricotta Toast
- Mexican Breakfast
- Carrot ginger soup with spicy shrimp
- Pesto Toastini
- Spicy broccoli and tofu
- Roasted cauliflower with spiced tomatoes
- Paprika shrimp with walnuts
- Banana Peach Sorbet
- Rhubarb Strawberry Compote
- Spiced roasted chickpeas
- Chocolate Coconut bites

 Vegetarian

 Vegan

Recipe Card

Name Of Recipe

Ingredients

- ☐
- ☐
- ☐
- ☐
- ☐
- ☐
- ☐
- ☐

Prep.Time

CookTime

Serves

| 2 | 4 | 6 | 8 |

Difficulty

★ ★ ★ ★ ★

DIRECTIONS

Grocery Shopping List

Name Of Category

Name Of Category

Name Of Category

Meal Planner

Dates

MONDAY

BREAKFAST	LUNCH	DINNER

TUESDAY

BREAKFAST	LUNCH	DINNER

WEDNESDAY

BREAKFAST	LUNCH	DINNER

THURSDAY

BREAKFAST	LUNCH	DINNER

FRIDAY

BREAKFAST	LUNCH	DINNER

SATURDAY

BREAKFAST	LUNCH	DINNER

SUNDAY

BREAKFAST	LUNCH	DINNER

www.cancerfreedomprogram.com

Dr. Amy

Cancer Expert - Cancer Survivor

Thank you!

What's Next?...

Now that you have taken the first step towards cancer recovery by including more healthy and nutritious foods, you may be wondering what the next steps are...

Because here's the deal - These recipes are super helpful but it's just a starting point in your recovery. If you really want to close the chapter on cancer, you probably already know you are going to need a little bit more support. I know recovery is scary. I've been there myself. But you can do this! I believe in you, thriver!

Apply HERE for The Cancer Freedom Program!

Click HERE
www.cancerfreedomprogram.com